CRYPTOCURRENCY

The Digital Future of Money

JACKSON GATES

INTRODUCTION

TABLE OF CONTENTS

Invest In Cryptocurrencies:
Chances And Risks

CHAPTER 11
Roles Of Virtual Currency In A
Cashless Society

CONCLUSION

INTRODUCTION

This is a basic overview and educational resource for an initial understanding of the concepts and principles behind cryptocurrencies. The purpose is to familiarize individuals with the basic aspects, functions and characteristics of digital currency.

Cryptocurrency refers to digital currency or a form of virtual currency that uses cryptography for secure financial transactions, controlling the creation of new entities, and validating asset transfers. Unlike traditional central bank currencies, cryptocurrencies are decentralized and based on a technology called blockchain, a distributed ledger that records all transactions on a computer network.

The purpose of an introduction to cryptocurrencies is to explain the underlying technology and the features that distinguish cryptocurrencies from traditional forms of money.
Describes cryptographic techniques used to secure transactions and ensure the integrity of currencies.

An overview of the distributed ledger technology that allows cryptocurrencies to work and record transactions transparently.
Introduces the concept of digital wallets. This is a software application for storing, managing and exchanging cryptocurrencies.

It describes the process of creating new cryptocurrency units through computation and how this contributes to the security and operation of blockchain networks.
This highlights the decentralized nature of cryptocurrencies,

eliminates the need for intermediaries such as banks, and enables peer-to-peer trading.

Learn about the importance of securing cryptocurrencies, including using private keys, two-factor authentication, and best practices to protect your digital assets.
Discover the many uses of cryptocurrencies beyond pure financial transactions.
Smart Contracts, Decentralized Finance (DeFi), and Potential Future Deployments. By providing an introductory understanding of cryptocurrencies, individuals gain insight into the potential

benefits and risks of this emerging technology.
This knowledge serves as a foundation for further exploring and participating in the cryptocurrency ecosystem as investors, developers and users of digital currencies.

CHAPTER 1
History And Development of Virtual Currency

Its purpose is to explore and understand the development and further development of digital currencies, also known as cryptocurrencies. This includes exploring the origins, milestones and transformations that have taken place in the world of cryptocurrencies.

Bitcoin was created by an anonymous individual or group named Satoshi Nakamoto who proposed a peer-to-peer electronic money system that relies on cryptography for secure transactions.

Since the introduction of Bitcoin, the cryptocurrency ecosystem has undergone significant development and growth. Numerous alternative cryptocurrencies, sometimes called altcoins, have been created, each with their own characteristics and use cases. The history and development of cryptocurrencies includes various aspects such as technological advances, regulatory developments, market trends, and community engagement. Cryptocurrencies are subject to significant price volatility and have attracted the attention of investors, traders, governments and the general public.

Over time, the underlying technology of cryptocurrencies, known as blockchain, has also evolved. Blockchain technology allows transactions to be recorded in a decentralized, secure and transparent manner, eliminating the need for intermediaries such as banks. There are other applications besides cryptocurrencies, such as supply chain management, voting systems, and decentralized finance (DeFi).

Moreover, the history and development of cryptocurrencies

are closely related to the regulatory framework. Governments and financial authorities around the world have adopted different approaches to address the challenges and opportunities of cryptocurrencies.

Regulatory debates and policies aim to strike a balance between promoting innovation and protecting consumers and the financial system. Studying the history and development of cryptocurrencies provides valuable insight into the development of this revolutionary form of digital assets. The focus is on the challenges, lessons learned and possible future directions of cryptocurrencies and the broader blockchain technology ecosystem.

Comprehensively examines the chronological development and transformation history of digital currencies, commonly referred to as cryptocurrencies. This area of research includes studying the origins of cryptocurrencies, major milestones, and the evolutionary changes that have shaped the cryptocurrency landscape.

The history of cryptocurrencies can be traced back to the late 2000s when the concept of Bitcoin was introduced by a person or group using the alias Satoshi Nakamoto. Bitcoin has emerged as a pioneer in decentralized digital currency, proposing a new peer-to-peer electronic money system that relies on cryptography to ensure secure and transparent *transactions. The publication of the Bitcoin Whitepaper in 2008 and the subsequent launch of the Bitcoin network in 2009 marked the beginning of a new era in digital finance.*

Since the introduction of Bitcoin, the cryptocurrency ecosystem has undergone remarkable growth and transformation. A variety of alternative cryptocurrencies, commonly known as altcoins, have emerged, each with their own characteristics, use cases, and underlying technology. Ethereum was born in his 2015, when Smarthe introduced the concept of contracts. This has enabled the development of decentralized applications (DApps), paving the way for the rise of blockchain-based platforms and tokens. The history and evolution of cryptocurrencies is marked by several important developments.

Technological advances are playing an important role, with innovation focused on improving scalability, privacy, and interoperability. The introduction of new consensus mechanisms like Proof of Stake (PoS) should eliminate energy consumption and scalability limitations associated with previous Proof of Work (PoW) based cryptocurrencies like Bitcoin.

Regulatory frameworks and government attitudes also have a significant impact on the development of cryptocurrencies. Initially, cryptocurrencies operated in a relatively unregulated environment, leading to rapid growth and adoption.

Regulatory frameworks and government attitudes also have a significant impact on the development of cryptocurrencies. Initially, cryptocurrencies operated in a relatively unregulated environment, leading to rapid growth and adoption.

However, as its popularity grew and concerns about money laundering, fraud and consumer protection grew, governments and financial authorities around the world began to develop regulations to address these issues. The regulatory landscape remains dynamic, with countries taking different approaches to cryptocurrency regulation, from outright bans to accepting cryptocurrencies as legal financial assets.

Additionally, the cryptocurrency market itself is subject to significant change. Significant price movements have taken place, attracting the attention of traders, investors and speculators. The emergence of cryptocurrency exchanges has made it easier to buy, sell and trade digital assets, contributing to market liquidity and accessibility. Moreover, the emergence of financial instruments such as futures contracts and exchange traded funds (ETFs) has further opened up opportunities for investors to participate in the cryptocurrency market.

The development of cryptocurrencies goes beyond their monetary value and technological advances. Blockchain technology, which is the foundation of virtual currency, is used in various industries and fields.

Its decentralized and immutable nature has led to its adoption in areas such as supply chain management, healthcare, voting systems and decentralized finance (DeFi). In particular, the DeFi sector has seen significant growth, enabling the construction of decentralized credit and lending platforms, decentralized exchanges, and other innovative financial services.

Studying the history and evolution of cryptocurrencies provides valuable insight into the evolution and maturation of this pioneering form of digital assets. It provides a comprehensive understanding of the challenges, lessons learned, and future opportunities of cryptocurrency and blockchain technology.

As interest and acceptance of cryptocurrencies grow, a deeper understanding of their history and evolution will be important for investors, policy makers and individuals seeking to navigate this rapidly evolving landscape. "The History and Evolution of Cryptocurrencies" examines the complex trajectories and multiple transformations that have shaped the emergence and evolution of digital currencies known as cryptocurrencies. This area of research includes an in-depth study of the historical origins of cryptocurrencies, key milestones, and the dynamic changes that have shaped the cryptocurrency landscape over time.

Sometimes called altcoins, these alternative digital currencies exhibit unique properties, capabilities and philosophies that expand the possibilities and uses of decentralized digital assets. It introduces the concept of smart contracts, enabling the creation of decentralized applications (DApps) and decentralized autonomous organizations (DAOs).

CHAPTER 2
How Blockchain Powers Cryptocurrencies

It refers to the underlying technologies and mechanisms that enable the existence and functioning of cryptocurrencies such as Bitcoin and Ethereum. It works on peer-to-peer networks and uses cryptography to ensure security and immutability.

A cryptocurrency is a digital or virtual currency that uses cryptography for secure financial transactions and controls the creation of additional entities. They use blockchain technology to enable peer-to-peer transactions without the need for intermediaries such as banks or governments.

How blockchain supports cryptocurrencies.
Blockchain eliminates the need for a central institution like a bank to process transactions. Instead, transactions are validated and recorded by network participants (nodes) distributed throughout the blockchain network. This decentralization ensures that no single entity can fully control the cryptocurrency system.

Every transaction on the blockchain network is recorded in a "block" and added to the chain of previous blocks. These blocks are publicly accessible, creating a transparent transaction history. This transparency helps prevent fraud and strengthens participant trust.

Blockchain uses cryptography to secure transactions. All transactions are digitally signed and cannot be tampered with or altered. Furthermore, due to its decentralized nature, blockchains are resistant to hacking attempts, as they require a majority of network participants to agree on transaction changes.

Once a transaction has been added to a block and recorded on the blockchain, it is virtually impossible to modify or remove it. This immutability ensures transaction history integrity and prevents double spending when the same cryptocurrency unit is used multiple times.

Blockchain networks use consensus mechanisms such as Proof of Work (PoW) and Proof of Stake (PoS) to validate and confirm transactions. These mechanisms ensure consistency among network participants and prevent fraudulent transactions from being included in the blockchain. In summary, blockchain technology advances cryptocurrencies by enabling decentralized, transparent, secure, and immutable transactions.

By enabling individuals to securely transfer digital assets without the need for

intermediaries, it will revolutionize the way financial transactions are thought and done.
Blockchain technology serves as the basis for the existence and functioning of cryptocurrencies. It is a distributed digital ledger that records and verifies transactions in a secure and transparent manner. Blockchain uses cryptography and computer networks to enable the creation, transmission, and storage of digital assets, including Bitcoin, Ethereum, and many other cryptocurrencies.

At its core, the blockchain functions as a decentralized system, eliminating the need for a central authority such as a bank or government to monitor and authenticate transactions. Instead, it is based on a network of participants, often called nodes, who collectively manage the blockchain and validate transactions performed on it.

One of the key features of blockchain technology is its transparency. Each transaction performed on the blockchain is recorded in a "block", which is then added to the chain of previous blocks to form an immutable history in chronological order of transactions.

This blockchain transparency allows anyone to see the details of a transaction, enhancing accountability and preventing fraud. Blockchain-based cryptocurrencies are protected by cryptography. Once a transaction is completed, it is digitally signed using complex mathematical algorithms to ensure the authenticity and integrity of transaction data. Additionally, the decentralized nature of blockchain makes it more resistant to hacking attempts and malicious activity.

CHAPTER 3
Advantages Of Cryptocurrencies Over Traditional Money

This refers to cryptocurrencies compared to traditional forms of money such as physical currencies.

A blockchain is a distributed ledger managed by a network of computers or nodes. This decentralized nature means that no single institution, such as a government or central bank, can fully control the currency. This feature improves transparency, security, and trust.

Cryptocurrencies use advanced cryptographic techniques to

*secure transactions and control
the creation of new entities.
Blockchain technology records
transactions in a tamper-proof
manner, making fraud and
tampering extremely difficult.
Additionally, the use of public key
cryptography provides strong
user authentication and
protection against identity theft.*

*Blockchain transactions are
recorded on a public ledger, but
most cryptocurrencies offer
varying degrees of privacy and
anonymity. Users can make
transactions without disclosing
personal information, thus
protecting against identity theft
and protecting financial privacy.*

Cryptocurrencies cross geographical borders and are accessible to anyone with an internet connection. This enables fast and convenient cross-border transactions without the need for intermediaries such as banks. Traditional banking systems often have limitations such as: By using cryptocurrencies, you can avoid business hours restrictions and high fees for international transfers.

Cryptocurrencies have the potential to provide financial services to people who are unbanked and lack access to traditional banking systems. With just a smartphone and internet access, individuals can participate in the cryptocurrency economy, opening up opportunities for financial inclusion and economic empowerment.

Cryptocurrency transactions typically have lower fees compared to traditional financial systems. Exchange Rate Fees, Transfer Fees and Brokerage Fees. Cryptocurrencies may offer a cheaper alternative.

Some cryptocurrencies, such as Ethereum, allow the creation of smart contracts. A smart contract is an auto-executing contract with predefined rules and conditions written in code. They automate transaction execution and can be used for a variety of applications including decentralized finance(DeFi), supply chain management, and more.

Cryptocurrencies and their underlying blockchain technology have the potential to revolutionize various industries, including finance, supply chain management, voting systems, intellectual property, and more. While cryptocurrencies have many advantages, it is important to note that they also come with their own challenges and risks, such as

Price Volatility, Regulatory Uncertainty, Scalability Issues, and Potential Illegal Activities. Therefore, it is important for individuals to exercise due diligence and caution when dealing with cryptocurrencies.

Cryptocurrencies work on a decentralized network, the so-called blockchain. Unlike traditional money, which is based on centralized institutions such as governments and central banks, cryptocurrencies are managed by computer networks and hubs spread all over the world. This decentralized nature eliminates middlemen and increases transparency as all transactions are recorded on a public ledger.

CHAPTER 4
Cryptocurrency Risks And Limitations

It is the potential downsides, challenges and vulnerabilities associated with the use and adoption of digital currencies such as Bitcoin, Ethereum and others. Although cryptocurrencies have some advantages, it is important to understand and consider the risks and limitations that come with them.

Cryptocurrencies are known for their large price fluctuations. Its value may fluctuate significantly in a short period of time, which may result in financial loss for investors and users.

The decentralized nature of cryptocurrencies means that they often operate outside of traditional financial regulations. This lack of oversight can make it difficult to address issues such as fraud, money laundering and market manipulation. Cryptocurrency transactions rely on cryptographic protocols to ensure security. However, the underlying technology and storage mechanisms can be vulnerable to hacking, theft, and fraud. Malicious attackers can target exchanges, wallets, or individual users to gain unauthorized access and steal digital assets.

As cryptocurrencies evolve, so do the legal frameworks and regulations in many jurisdictions. This uncertainty can create tax, compliance and legal protection challenges for businesses and individuals.

Concerns remain about the scalability of the blockchain network that underlies most cryptocurrencies. Increased trading volume can cause problems such as network congestion, slow transaction processing times, and increased transaction fees.

The user experience when dealing with cryptocurrencies can be complicated and intimidating for beginners. A lack of intuitive interfaces and user-friendly tools can limit mainstream adoption and usability.

Once a cryptocurrency transaction is confirmed on the blockchain, it is usually irreversible. While this feature provides security, it can cause problems if transactions are sent to the wrong address or fraudulent activity is committed.

Some cryptocurrencies, such as Bitcoin, are based on an energy-intensive mining process. The high energy consumption associated with mining has an impact on the environment and can lead to increased CO2 emissions.

Cryptocurrency markets are prone to manipulation and speculative trading practices. Prices are relatively illiquid and unregulated, and can be easily manipulated, leading to significant price volatility and potential financial losses. Despite the growing popularity of cryptocurrencies, their acceptance as a mainstream payment method remains limited. Factors such as the limited number of traders, lack of awareness, and awareness of volatility and risk are hindering widespread adoption.

Understanding these risks and limitations can help individuals, businesses and policy makers make informed decisions and develop strategies to reap the benefits of cryptocurrencies while mitigating potential downsides.

Cryptocurrencies are known for their large price fluctuations. Cryptocurrency values can fluctuate dramatically in short periods of time, making them highly unpredictable as an investment asset. This volatility presents a risk to investors as it can result in significant gains or losses depending on market conditions.

Cryptocurrencies operate outside traditional financial regulations.

This decentralized nature brings benefits such as privacy and freedom from government control, but it also brings challenges. A lack of regulatory oversight can lead to problems such as fraud, market manipulation and money laundering, which can affect market stability and investor protection.

Cryptocurrency transactions rely on cryptographic protocols to ensure security. However, the underlying technology and storage mechanisms can be vulnerable to hacking, theft, and fraud.

CHAPTER 5
Types Of Cryptocurrencies Currently Available

It refers to the various digital or virtual currencies currently in existence. Cryptocurrencies are decentralized digital assets that use cryptography to secure transactions, control the creation of new entities, and verify asset transfers. The concept of cryptocurrency started with Bitcoin in 2009, but it has since expanded and today there are many types of cryptocurrencies with different functions, purposes and underlying technologies.

It operates on a peer-to-peer network and is based on blockchain technology providing a decentralized and transparent system for transactions and asset storage.

Its native cryptocurrency, Ether, will be used to facilitate transactions and incentivize participants on the Ethereum network.

It aims to enable fast and cheap international money transfers and is widely used for cross-border transactions by banks and financial institutions.

Litecoin is often thought of as the "lite" version of Bitcoin. It offers faster transaction confirmation times and different hashing algorithms, making it more suitable for everyday transactions.

Bitcoin Cash is a fork of Bitcoin that aims to solve the scalability problem. This increases the block size limit, allowing each block to handle more transactions. Polkadot is a multi-chain platform that allows different blockchains to work together and share information. The aim is to build a scalable and networked blockchain ecosystem.

This will be used to pay trading fees on the platform and

participate in token sales on the Binance Launchpad.

Stellar is a platform for fast and cheap cross-border payments. The aim is to network financial institutions and enable remittances around the world.

Originally invented as a hoax, his Dogecoin grew in popularity and built a dedicated community. It is often used for tips and charitable donations, but is also known for its speculative value.

These are just a few examples of the variety of cryptocurrencies available today. Each cryptocurrency has its own set of features, use cases, and underlying technologies that *serve different needs and preferences within the digital currency ecosystem.*

It operates on a decentralized network called blockchain that guarantees transaction transparency and security. Bitcoin's main function is to act as a digital currency for peer-to-peer transactions, store of value, and investment. It is widely accepted as a digital asset and recognized as a potential alternative to traditional fiat currency.

CHAPTER 6
Buy, Sell And Store Cryptocurrencies

Buying, selling, and storing cryptocurrencies refers to various activities related to acquiring, trading, and securing digital currencies.
When purchasing cryptocurrencies, digital currencies are purchased using traditional fiat currencies.

This can also be done through online cryptocurrency exchanges, peer-to-peer platforms, or directly by individuals and companies wishing to sell their digital assets. Typically, a buyer creates an account on a cryptocurrency exchange, deposits funds, and uses that money to buy the desired amount of cryptocurrency at prevailing market rates.

Selling cryptocurrency means exchanging digital currency for fiat currency or other cryptocurrencies. Those who own digital assets can sell them through cryptocurrency exchanges and peer-to-peer platforms. This process involves choosing a cryptocurrency to sell, specifying a desired selling price or assuming the current *market price, and initiating trading.*

Cryptocurrency storage is the storage of digital assets in a secure digital wallet. A cryptocurrency wallet is a software application, physical device, or online service that allows users to store, manage, and manipulate digital currency. A wallet consists of two cryptographic keys.

A public key that acts as a wallet address for receiving funds and a private key that provides access to stored cryptocurrencies. Wallets can be classified as hot wallets. Storing cryptocurrencies

in wallets allows users to manage their assets and protect them from potential security threats.

Overall, buying, selling and storing cryptocurrencies is an integral part of participating in the digital currency ecosystem. These activities allow individuals and businesses to acquire, trade and protect their holdings, reflecting the dynamic nature of the cryptocurrency market. user.

When purchasing cryptocurrencies, digital currencies are purchased using traditional fiat currencies. The primary way to buy cryptocurrencies is through online cryptocurrency exchanges. These platforms act as intermediaries, connecting buyers and sellers and facilitating the exchange of digital assets. To buy cryptocurrencies, individuals typically create an account with a reputable exchange, go through the required verification procedures, and fund the account.

Cryptocurrency sale refers to the process of exchanging digital currency for fiat currency or other cryptocurrencies. Similar to buying cryptocurrency, selling cryptocurrency is typically done through a cryptocurrency exchange or peer-to-peer platform. When selling cryptocurrencies, individuals must select the specific digital asset they wish to sell, specify their desired sale price or accept the current market price, and initiate the transaction.

The cryptocurrency is then transferred from the seller's wallet to the buyer's wallet, and the seller receives the agreed currency or cryptocurrency in return.

Some exchanges also offer the ability to place limit or stop orders during sales, allowing users to set specific terms of sale. It is important to note that the sale of cryptocurrencies may be subject to taxation and therefore individuals must comply with the relevant regulations of their jurisdiction.

Cryptocurrency storage is the storage of digital assets in a secure digital wallet. A cryptocurrency wallet is a software application, physical device, or online service that allows users to store, manage, and manipulate digital currency. The wallet uses cryptographic algorithms to generate two types of keys. public and private keys. Public keys, also known as wallet addresses, are used to receive funds, while private keys are required to access and manage stored cryptocurrency.

Hot wallets are connected to the internet and are suitable for storing small amounts of cryptocurrency as they provide convenient access for frequent transactions. A cold wallet, on the other hand, is an offline device or paper-based solution that enhances security by keeping private keys offline. They are often used for long-term storage *of large amounts of cryptocurrency. Use strong passwords, enable two-factor authentication, and regularly back up your wallet data.*

CHAPTER 7
The Use Of Cryptocurrency Mining

It refers to the process by which transactions are validated and validated on the blockchain network and added to the public ledger of the blockchain. It is a key component of many cryptocurrencies, including Bitcoin and Ethereum, and serves multiple purposes such as maintaining network security, issuing new coins, and facilitating transactions.

The mining process uses powerful computers or special mining hardware to solve complex mathematical puzzles and algorithms. Miners compete to be the first to solve these puzzles and earn rewards in the form of newly minted cryptocurrency coins.

Miners collect pending transactions from the network and verify their authenticity and validity. Make sure the sender has sufficient funds, the transactions are not duplicated, and the rules of the network are being followed.

Valid transactions are grouped into blocks. Each block contains a unique identifier called a "hash" and a reference to the hash of the previous block, creating a chain of blocks called a blockchain.

Miners must find solutions to cryptographic puzzles that require large amounts of computing power and energy consumption. This process is called proof of work. Miners continuously guess random numbers, so-called nonces, to find hash values that meet certain criteria. The winning miner who finds the correct nonce first gets a reward.

When a miner finds a solution, it submits it to the network. Other miners then validate the solutions and transactions within the block. If the majority of miners agree that the solution is correct, the block is considered valid and added to the blockchain.

The crypto puzzle difficulty is adjusted regularly to keep the block creation rate constant. As more miners join the network, it becomes more difficult to prevent blocks from being rapidly mined. Conversely, when miners leave the network, the difficulty of maintaining block creation rates decreases. It is important to note that cryptocurrency mining requires large amounts of computing resources and energy consumption.

Some cryptocurrencies, such as Bitcoin, have become increasingly resource intensive, raising concerns about their environmental impact. As a result, alternative consensus mechanisms such as Proof of Stake have emerged to address these issues.

CHAPTER 8
Impact Of Cryptocurrencies On The Global Economy

Cryptocurrencies are decentralized digital assets that use cryptography for secure financial transactions and are based on a technology called blockchain. This emerging currency format, represented by well-known examples such as Bitcoin and Ethereum, has gained significant attention and acceptance in recent years, transforming many aspects of the global economy.

The impact of cryptocurrencies on the global economy can be

analyzed from multiple perspectives.
Cryptocurrencies have the potential to provide financial services to people around the world who are unbanked or underbanked. By leveraging blockchain technology, cryptocurrencies enable secure and low-cost transactions, eliminating the need for traditional bank intermediaries.

This improved financial inclusion can empower individuals and businesses in developing countries, boost economic growth and reduce inequality.

The decentralized nature of cryptocurrencies poses challenges to traditional centralized financial systems such as banks and governments. Cryptocurrencies operate independently of central authorities, giving individuals direct control over their funds and eliminating the need for intermediaries for transactions. This disruption could lead to shifts in power dynamics, altering traditional mechanisms of monetary policy, financial regulation and governance.

Cryptocurrencies have become an attractive asset class for investors and speculators. High yields, volatility, and the potential emergence of new investment vehicles have attracted significant attention from both retail and institutional investors. However, the speculative nature of cryptocurrencies also poses risks such as market volatility and regulatory uncertainty that could affect global financial stability.

The development of cryptocurrencies has spurred innovation in various fields, especially blockchain technology. Blockchain has the potential to revolutionize not only the financial industry, but also supply chains, healthcare, voting *systems, and more. These technological advances could lead to greater efficiency, transparency and security in many areas of the global economy.*

The rise of cryptocurrencies poses regulatory and legal challenges for governments and policymakers around the world. Authorities struggle with the need to strike a balance between promoting innovation and ensuring consumer protection, preventing money laundering and fighting illegal activity. The regulatory landscape surrounding cryptocurrencies varies from country to country, resulting in a complex and evolving environment that can affect the adoption and integration of cryptocurrencies into the global economy.

The impact of cryptocurrencies on the global economy is multifaceted and includes financial inclusion, disruption of traditional systems, investment opportunities, innovation and regulatory challenges. As cryptocurrencies evolve and become more accepted, their impact on the global economy will grow, shaping the future of finance and technology. Cryptocurrency, a type of digital currency based on blockchain technology, has emerged as a disruptive force in the global economy.

Its decentralized nature, secure transactions, and financial inclusion potential have attracted a great deal of attention and acceptance in recent years. This article examines the various impacts of cryptocurrencies on the global economy and their potential for financial inclusion, disruption of traditional financial systems, investment opportunities, innovation, and related regulatory challenges.

One of the most significant impacts of cryptocurrency is its potential to promote financial inclusion. Cryptocurrencies using blockchain technology offer people without access to traditional banking services the opportunity to make secure and

*cheap transactions.
Cryptocurrencies offer a financial alternative in developing countries where the majority of the population is unbanked or only banked.*

CHAPTER 9
Virtual Currency Regulations and Future Prospects

This refers to our understanding and analysis of cryptocurrency rules, policies and legal frameworks, as well as the anticipated trends and opportunities regarding the future development and adoption of digital currencies.

Laws, regulations and policies issued by governments and regulators governing the use, trading and issuance of virtual currency. Governments around the world are grappling with the need to create regulatory frameworks that balance innovation and consumer protection. These regulations often cover areas such as anti-money laundering (AML), know your customer (KYC) requirements, tax, securities regulation, and investor protection.

It refers to the trends, opportunities and challenges anticipated in digital currency. Factors such as technological advances, market acceptance, regulatory developments, institutional engagement, public sentiment and economic impact are considered. The forward-looking outlook aims to provide

insight into the potential growth,
stability and impact of
cryptocurrencies on various
sectors including finance,
technology and the global
economy.

Understanding cryptocurrency
regulation and future prospects is
crucial for individuals,
businesses, investors and policy
makers. This will help you
navigate the legal and regulatory
landscape surrounding
cryptocurrencies and make
informed decisions about your
involvement in this rapidly
evolving industry. In addition,
analyzing the future outlook will
enable stakeholders to assess

potential risks and opportunities associated with cryptocurrencies, adjust strategies, and effectively position themselves in the market. It provides an in-depth survey of the legal frameworks, policies, and guidance governing the use, trading, and issuance of digital currencies, providing comprehensive forecast trends, opportunities, and forecasts. The challenges facing the cryptocurrency ecosystem are pressing.

Given the decentralized and borderless nature of digital currencies, governments around the world have grappled with the need to create regulatory frameworks that balance innovation and consumer protection. These regulations cover a wide range of areas including, but not limited to, anti-money laundering (AML) and know your customer (KYC) requirements, tax regulations, securities regulations, consumer protection measures, and prevention of illegal activity.

The regulatory landscape for cryptocurrencies varies greatly from country to country, with some countries approving and supporting the technology, while others have imposed severe restrictions or outright banned it. Understanding the regulatory environment is critical for individuals and businesses involved in cryptocurrency activities as it helps them comply with their legal obligations, ensure the security of their operations.

A cryptocurrency outlook refers to a detailed analysis and forecast of the trends, opportunities and challenges that may affect the development and adoption of digital currencies. This includes various factors that influence the development of cryptocurrencies, such as technological advancements, market dynamics, regulatory developments, institutional initiatives, public sentiment, and macroeconomic factors.

Technological advances will play a major role in shaping the future of cryptocurrencies. Innovations such as scalability solutions, privacy improvements, and interoperability protocols can have a significant impact on the usability and efficiency of digital currencies.

CHAPTER 10
Invest In Cryptocurrencies: Chance And Risk

Opportunity and risk refers to the process of allocating financial resources to digital currencies as a means of potentially generating profits. This term includes the advantages and disadvantages associated with participating in this particular form of investment.

Opportunities to invest in cryptocurrencies have the potential for huge financial returns. Cryptocurrencies such as Bitcoin and Ethereum have historically experienced significant price increases, resulting in significant returns for early investors. The decentralized nature of cryptocurrencies gives you the opportunity to diversify your investment portfolio. Additionally, the emerging blockchain technology behind cryptocurrencies presents opportunities for innovation and disruption in many industries.

However, in addition to opportunities, investing in cryptocurrencies also comes with some risks that investors should be aware of. High volatility in the cryptocurrency market can cause sharp price fluctuations, resulting in significant financial losses. Regulatory uncertainty can also affect markets and investor sentiment as governments around the world struggle to shape cryptocurrencies. Additionally, the prevalence of fraud and fraud in the cryptocurrency space poses risks to investors who may fall victim to such schemes.

Additionally, investing in cryptocurrencies requires a thorough understanding of the technology, market dynamics, and associated risks. Lack of knowledge and wrong decisions can lead to financial setbacks. Another issue is security, as the digital nature of cryptocurrencies makes them vulnerable to hacking and theft if proper precautions are not taken.

It highlights the various risks and challenges, as well as the potential economic benefits associated with investing in digital currencies. We emphasize the importance of conducting thorough research, understanding the risks involved and making informed decisions when entering the cryptocurrency market. Investing in cryptocurrencies has received a lot of attention in recent years as digital currencies have emerged as an alternative asset class.

This explores the different landscapes surrounding this form of investment and examines both the potential benefits and inherent risks that investors should consider before entering the cryptocurrency market.

Cryptocurrencies such as Bitcoin and Ethereum have experienced significant price increases over the years. Early investors in these digital assets have made significant returns, making cryptocurrency investments an attractive option for individuals looking for a high return on investment.

Cryptocurrencies offer an opportunity to diversify investment portfolios beyond traditional asset classes such as stocks and bonds. This diversification reduces overall investment risk and increases long-term growth potential.

The technology underlying cryptocurrencies, known as blockchain, has the potential to revolutionize many industries. By investing in cryptocurrencies, investors can participate in the transformative potential of decentralized systems and benefit from the advancements and innovations made possible by blockchain technology.

The cryptocurrency market is notorious for its high volatility as prices fluctuate dramatically in short periods of time. This inherent volatility poses a significant risk to investors as it can lead to significant financial losses if not managed carefully.

Governments and regulators around the world are still struggling with the crypto regulatory framework. Any potential regulatory change, ban or restrictive policy could have a material impact on the cryptocurrency market, creating *uncertainty and undermining investor confidence.*

The digital nature of cryptocurrencies exposes investors to security risks such as hacking, fraud and theft. The prevalence of crypto-related fraud and vulnerabilities in online wallets and exchanges highlights the importance of robust security measures and vigilance to protect your investments.

CHAPTER 11
Role Of Virtual Currency In A Cashless Society

The Role of Cryptocurrencies in a Cashless Society examines the importance and impact of digital currencies in an economy where physical cash transactions are declining or disappearing. A cashless society is characterized by a departure from traditional banknotes and coins, and most financial transactions are conducted electronically.

Cryptocurrencies such as Bitcoin, Ethereum and Litecoin are decentralized digital currencies that use cryptography to control secure transactions and the creation of new entities. They use a technology called blockchain, a distributed ledger that records all transactions on a computer network.

In a cashless society, cryptocurrencies will play an important role by providing an alternative means of conducting financial transactions. Cryptocurrencies facilitate peer-to-peer digital transactions, allowing individuals to send and receive funds directly without intermediaries such as banks or payment processors. This could streamline the payment process, *reduce transaction costs, and increase efficiency.*

Cryptocurrencies use robust cryptographic techniques to ensure the security and integrity of transactions. These give individuals more control over their financial information and can offer enhanced privacy features compared to traditional banking systems. Financial Inclusion:

Cryptocurrencies have the potential to promote financial inclusion by providing access to financial services to the unbanked. With a smartphone and an internet connection, individuals can participate in the cryptocurrency ecosystem and securely store, send and receive funds.

Cryptocurrencies cross geographic boundaries and facilitate cross-border transactions. Traditional international money transfer methods are often subject to high fees, delays and brokerage fees. Cryptocurrencies enable faster and cheaper cross-border transactions, benefiting both businesses and individuals.

Cryptocurrencies and their underlying blockchain technology have fostered innovation in various fields. Smart contracts, decentralized finance (DeFi), and non-fungible tokens (NFTs) are examples of new applications emerging and transforming industries such as finance, supply chain management, and the arts.

While cryptocurrencies have many advantages, there are also challenges to consider, such as: B. Price volatility, regulatory framework, scalability and energy consumption. Additionally, the transition to a cashless society must address issues of security, trust and accessibility for those who do not have access to technology or face barriers to digital currency adoption.

The role of virtual currency in a cashless society is wide-ranging. They provide a safe, efficient and comprehensive means to conduct digital transactions, cross borders, foster innovation and disrupt traditional financial systems. However, it is important to address the challenges associated with the introduction of a cashless society and ensure that all sectors of society can reap the benefits of a cashless society.

CONCLUSION

Cryptocurrency was a groundbreaking innovation that revolutionized the traditional financial system and the way we perceive and interact with money. Virtual currency has continued to grow since its birth and continues to spread remarkably all over the world.

The decentralized nature of cryptocurrencies, enabled by blockchain technology, has enabled levels of transparency, security and accessibility previously unthinkable in traditional financial systems. Cryptocurrencies allow individuals to directly control their finances without the need for intermediaries such as banks or governments.

This has given people around the world, especially those in underserved regions, the opportunity to participate in the global economy and access financial services. Moreover, the underlying blockchain technology has been shown to have potential applications in various industries beyond cryptocurrencies. Blockchain has paved the way for the development of smart contracts, decentralized applications and asset tokenization. These innovations promise greater efficiency, reduced fraud and greater transparency in areas such as supply chain management, healthcare and voting systems.

However, it is important to recognize that the cryptocurrency landscape is not without challenges. Volatility, regulatory uncertainty, security risks, and scalability concerns are areas that require continued attention and development. As the cryptocurrency ecosystem evolves, industry players, policymakers and regulators will work together to create a balanced framework that protects consumer interests and fosters innovation while maintaining market stability.

Despite these challenges, the potential of cryptocurrencies and blockchain technology remains immense. Continuous advances in research and development and increasing acceptance by institutions suggest that cryptocurrencies are becoming ubiquitous. They have become an integral part of the global financial ecosystem and will continue to shape the future of finance, business and technology. Looking ahead, it will be crucial to harness the transformative power of cryptocurrencies while ensuring responsible use, informed decision-making and the continued evolution of the regulatory framework.

In this way, we can harness the full potential of cryptocurrencies to drive financial inclusion, economic empowerment, and technological progress for the benefit of individuals and societies around the world. Digital currency has emerged as a disruptive innovation that will turn the traditional financial system upside down and revolutionize the way we perceive and interact with money. Since the birth of Bitcoin in 2009, virtual currencies have continued to grow and continue to spread remarkably around the world.

The decentralized nature of cryptocurrencies, enabled by

blockchain technology, has enabled levels of transparency, security and accessibility previously unthinkable in traditional financial systems. By using cryptographic principles and distributed ledgers, cryptocurrencies do not require intermediaries such as banks or governments to facilitate transactions. This not only streamlines the process, but also puts individuals in direct control of their finances.

One of the main advantages of cryptocurrencies is their potential to provide financial services to disadvantaged people around the world. Traditional banking services are often inaccessible or inconvenient for people in developing countries and remote areas. Cryptocurrencies can fill this gap by enabling secure, low-cost transactions without the need for physical infrastructure. This could open up economic opportunities to promote financial inclusion and empower individuals previously excluded from the formal financial system. Moreover, the underlying blockchain technology has been shown to have potential applications in various industries beyond cryptocurrencies.

Blockchain has paved the way for the development of smart contracts, decentralized applications (dApps) and asset tokenization. Smart contracts, self-executing contracts with clauses written directly in code, have the potential to automate and streamline complex processes across industries, from supply chain management to real estate transactions. Moreover, decentralized applications based on blockchain technology can disrupt centralized applications.

Moreover, decentralized applications built on blockchain technology have the potential to disrupt centralized systems and facilitate peer-to-peer interactions. These dApps increase data protection, security and transparency, creating new business models and opportunities. Furthermore, asset tokenization, where physical assets are represented by digital tokens on the blockchain, will revolutionize traditional financial markets by increasing liquidity, reducing intermediaries and enabling fractional ownership.

However, it is important to recognize that the cryptocurrency landscape is not without challenges. Volatility, regulatory uncertainty, security risks, and scalability concerns are areas that require continued attention and development. The high volatility of cryptocurrencies has raised concerns about their suitability as stable stores of value or mediums of exchange. Additionally, the cryptocurrency regulatory environment is still evolving, with jurisdictions taking different approaches. Finding a balance between innovation and consumer protection remains a key challenge for policymakers and regulators.

Additionally, the security of cryptocurrencies and blockchain networks is paramount. While the underlying blockchain technology is robust and tamper-proof, individual users should take care to protect their digital assets from cyber threats and fraud. Education and awareness about best practices for custody and protection of cryptocurrencies is critical to the widespread adoption and trust of these digital assets.

Furthermore, the scalability of blockchain networks, especially in terms of transaction throughput and energy efficiency, is an ongoing challenge. As cryptocurrencies grow in popularity, the need for scalable and eco-friendly solutions becomes even greater. Researchers and developers are actively looking for solutions such as improving layer 2 protocols, sharding, and consensus algorithms to address these scalability issues. Despite these challenges, the potential of cryptocurrencies and blockchain technology remains immense. Continuous advances in research and development and increasing acceptance by institutions suggest that cryptocurrencies are becoming ubiquitous. They have become an integral part of the global financial ecosystem and will continue to shape the future of finance, business and technology.

Looking ahead, it will be crucial to harness the transformative power of cryptocurrencies while ensuring responsible use, informed decision-making and the continued evolution of the regulatory framework. Cooperation among industry players, policy makers and regulators is essential to create a balanced framework that fosters innovation while protecting consumer interests and maintaining market stability. By addressing challenges such as volatility, regulatory clarity, security and scalability, we can unlock the full potential of cryptocurrencies.